THE SPANISH MISSIONS OF CALIFORNIA

🖐 A procession led by Spanish priests, called padres, celebrates the establishment of a mission in California. Each mission built along the unsettled coast of California spawned small colonies that grew into cities such as San Diego and San Francisco.

THE AMERICAN WEST

THE SPANISH MISSIONS OF CALIFORNIA

ROB STAEGER

MASON CREST PUBLISHERS

Dedication:
To my own mother. For her faith, and her faith in me.

Mason Crest Publishers
370 Reed Road
Broomall PA 19008
www.masoncrest.com

First printing

1 3 5 7 9 8 6 4 2

Library of Congress Cataloging-in-Publication Data
on file at the Library of Congress

ISBN 1-59084-059-3

Publisher's note: many of the quotations in this book come from
original sources, and contain the spelling and grammatical
inconsistencies of the original text.

CONTENTS

👆 Native Californians garbed in ritual dress meet Father Garzes, one of the padres concerned with changing the ways of the natives. Soon after the Spaniards arrived in California, the clash between their culture and that of the natives that lived in the land became apparent.

THE MARCH TO SAN DIEGO

TRAVELING WAS NOT EASY FOR FATHER JUNIPERO SERRA. HE WAS TOUGH AND DETERMINED, and he had a lot of energy for a 55-year-old. But he also had a crippled leg, and he was marching hundreds of miles to San Diego.

Father Serra's leg had been injured 20 years before. It was in 1749, during his first weeks in Mexico. His ship from Spain had landed in Vera Cruz. Serra walked the 550 miles to Mexico City. On the way, a spider bit him on his leg. The spider's poison was powerful. His leg swelled up and never fully healed. It had hurt to walk ever since.

And yet, Father Serra walked. His job was too important to stop. Mexico's top official, José de Gálvez, had met with him in Santa Ana. During their meeting, Gálvez gave him an important task. Serra was to found two missions in California. One would be in San Diego, and the other would be in Monterey. His work would be important to Spain, and important to God. Father Serra had been working in missions for 20 years, but this was different. This was starting a mission in unknown territory. Up until now, he had been continuing the work of others. In California, he would truly make his mark.

Captain Juan de Portola would help him. Portola had been walking even farther than Father Serra had. The captain had come from the south, leading soldiers and some converted Indians. Father Serra joined Portola's group in Velicata. They left, heading north, on May 15.

Portola's group wasn't the only one going to San Diego. Two ships were also sailing there, and there was a cattle drive ahead of them. All three groups would get to San Diego before them. Everyone expected the mission to be well under way by the time Father Serra arrived.

The cattle drive cleared their trail. However, the men and livestock ate and drank most of the nearby food and water. Because of this, Portola's group often had very little to eat. At one point, some of them ate mules to survive.

There was one bright spot in the journey. Father Serra saw someone applying an ointment to a pack mule's saddle sores. Serra tried the ointment for his inflamed leg, and it eased his pain a great deal.

About a week away from San Diego, most of the converted Indians deserted the group. Many others had died along the way. Hungry and exhausted, Father Serra's expedition arrived on July 1, 1769. Only half of the original group had made it.

They found no relief in San Diego. No mission was being

built. Most of the sailors were dead from scurvy. Half of the colonists were too sick to stand. Their supply ship hadn't arrived, so they had very little food, and they were surrounded by thousands of California Indians. The California mission system would be the hardest thing Father Serra had ever tried. The march to San Diego was just the beginning.

Passage by land *to* CALIFORNIA
Discover'd by Father Eusebius
Francis Kino *a Jesuit*;
between the Years 1698, & 1701:
containing likewise the
New Missions *of the* Jesuits.

5   10   15   20 Leagues

35

34

33

32

31

30

29

28

27

26

Rio Colorado or of the North

Alchedomas

A Great Mountain which extend

Blue R.

NEW MEXI

Rio Azul

Casa
Grande

Cutganes 1701

S.t Dionysio
1700

S.t Matthew de Licori

S.t Andree de Balqui

S.t Phillip

la Sola

S.t James
de Oiadaibuise

S.t Angelo

S.t Ca

therin

S.t Paul

S.t Peter
1690

S.t Matthias de
Tucomagoidag

S.t Simon
de Tucsan

S.t Boniface

S.t Cosnie

S.t A

Hoabonoma

Yumas

Cocomaricopas

S.t Francis

S.t Seraphin

S.t Francois

Xa
du Ba

la Tinaxa

Agua escondida

Aguage de la Luna

la Merced

S.t Gaet

Bagiopas

Carizal

S.t Marcel

S.t Raphael

PIMERIA

S.t Gue

Medanos
de Aren

M. de S.t Claire
3 Ojtos 1698

S.t Louis de Bacapa

S.te Eulalie

Susonic

Aguimuri

Sierra Azul
The Blue Mountain

Bategui

S.t Edonard de
Baipia Addi

Tubutama

Cocospara

Quiquimas

Sierra Nevada

Sobas

Himares
Tupo

Res

Mountain
cover'd
with Snow

S.t Mark

Conception del
Cabeca

S.t Antoine
d'Uguitoa

S.t Ignatius
Dolores

Navareno

S.t Diegue
de Pitquin

S.t Magdalena

S.t Matthew

R. de S.t Ignatii

Topoquis

Opodepe

Nacameri

SONOR

SEA

Ponulo

OF

S.t John

P. de S.t Sabine

Angeles
Bay of
S.t John Sobas

S.t Xavier

S.t Mi

S.ta Rosalia
S.t Antony

I. S.t Augustin

Baptist

R. de Sonora

Tecorina
Comoripa

Isles of Salt

P. de
S.t Xavier

Guaimas

Hiaquim

Ca
Bacum
Torim
Bicam

The Virgins
or las Vierges

R.t Christopher

B. des Balenes
or of Whales

PART

OF

CALIFORNIA

Beten

R. d'Hiaque

Rahum Potam

P. de S.t Martin

R. de Mayo

NEW

MAYO

Vechejoa

S.t Croix

Guimies

S.t Jean de Londo

F. Bruno

Coronados

P. de
S.t Xavier

CALIFORNI

B. S.t Luke

Thebaida
Reyes

S.t Isidoro

S.t Nicholas

Loreto

Carmen

Mach

B. des Sable
or of Sand

S.t Stephen

S.t John

las S.S. Innocents

Santiago
S.t James

Nochebuena

Concho

S.t Xavier
de Biaundo

Giganta

Port de Danzantes

Farellon

B.

SOUTH SEA

P. of the New Year
discovered
1685.

Rio de S.t Thomas

Edues

Port de Matanzas

Yodivineage

B. Bowen S.t

A

MOUNTAINS WHICH REACH THE HEAVENS

IN THE MIDDLE OF THE 18TH CENTURY, CALIFORNIA WAS CONSIDERED A SPANISH territory. Much of what Europeans called the "New World" was Spain's. Spanish explorers scoured the earth in search of riches. Finding silk, pearls, or gold, they claimed each place for Spain.

Spain sent colonists to wherever it claimed. There was one exception—California. Spain had claimed it in the middle of the 16th century, but sent no one to live there. There were several reasons for this. First, California had mountains all along its coast. They could make colonization difficult. Also, Europeans thought that California was an island. This made the mountains seem even more threatening. Finally, there were

🐦 This map illustrates the route taken by Father Eusebio Francisco Kino. His travels proved that California was not an island, as previously assumed, but a peninsula.

11

Originally, Spanish colonists believed California was an island, and the maps of the time reflected this belief. Eusebio Kino and Juan Salvaterria changed that when they walked across the Baja. Along the way, they saw that the Sea of Cortes came to an end, meaning that water didn't surround the land. Once they realized their maps were in error, they knew it would be possible to colonize the area by land.

legends of fierce, dark-skinned warriors there, ruled by Queen Califa. None of these "facts" made Spaniards eager to settle in California. Spain would need a very good reason to send a **colony** there.

In fact, not much at all was known about California. In 200 years, Spain had sent only two sea expeditions to explore the California coast. Juan Rodriguez Cabrillo headed the first, in 1542. With his ships, the *San Salvador* and the *Victoria*, Cabrillo mapped most of the coastline. He wrote, "There are mountains which seem to reach the heavens, and the sea beats on them … it appears as though they would fall on the ships." This description did little to encourage colonists.

Sixty years later, Captain Sebastian Vizcaino led another voyage. He named many of California's bays and ports. Most of them were named after saints—San Diego, San Francisco, and others. But Vizcaino named one northern port after his wealthy sponsor, the count of Monte Rey. To impress the count, he described the port of Monterey as nearly perfect. He exaggerated its virtues and played down its faults. This little white lie would come back to haunt the Spanish.

A Spaniard didn't make the other recorded trip to California. It was made by Sir Francis Drake. The English captain landed near San Francisco in 1579. There, he encountered the coastal Miwok people. It was a strange and disturbing meeting. The Indians brought Drake's crew gifts, but when Drake offered gifts in return, they refused. Also, the Indian women walked, crying, among the sailors. Drake described them "weeping and tearing their flesh." He assumed that the Miwok thought the Europeans were gods. Drake thought he convinced the Miwok king to swear allegiance to England. He claimed California for England, calling it New Albion.

Drake had completely misunderstood the situation. For one thing, the "king" he had spoken to was a local chief. The California Indians had no king. They just had local leaders. Secondly, although the sailors amazed the Miwok, no one thought they were gods. The truth was even stranger. They thought the Europeans were the walking dead! In Miwok legends, the land of the dead was in the West—the same place the English had sailed from. The sailors' pale skin clinched it. They were from somewhere beyond this life. The Miwok gave offerings to the spirits to keep them happy. But they wanted no souvenirs from beyond the grave.

At the time, what we know as California was called **Alta**, or upper, **California**. Below it is a peninsula called **Baja**, or lower,

👆 A cross embellishes the grounds of the San Diego mission. Though not all Native Americans understood the concept behind the cross, they recognized that to Christians it was a powerful spiritual symbol.

California. Spanish colonization of the area began in Baja. For years, the Spanish had been trying to settle in the arid region. They had little success. In 1683, they started a colony in La Paz, on Baja's southern tip. The first two years at La Paz were devastating. There was drought, starvation, and plague. Eventually, the colony was abandoned. Two **Jesuit missionaries** stayed behind. Eusebio Kino and his friend, Juan Salvaterria, walked across Baja. Moving northward, they blazed a long trail. It came to be known as *El Camino del Diablo*—The

Devil's Road. Eventually, Father Kino made his way into what we know as California. There, he saw the Sea of Cortés end. The words in his journal were plain and true: *California no es isla.* (California is not an island.) Despite a century of faulty maps, it would be possible to colonize the area by land.

The expansion of Spanish missions into Alta (upper) California was the result of King Charles III's desire to protect Spain's interests from Russian fur trappers. The trappers had been spotted hunting on the Farallone Islands near San Francisco.

In order to make the missions work, the Jesuits created the Pious Fund. The fund was made up of private donations. In Kino's time, it rose to $200,000. Father Kino was able to found 29 missions throughout Baja California.

One of the biggest problems the Spanish colonies faced was communication. The colonies were governed by officials called **viceroys**. The viceroys had little decision-making power. Each viceroy had to answer to the king. The problem was, any questions took more than a year to reach Spain and be answered. So, the answers became very long and involved, to cover every possibility. They were sometimes as long as books.

In spite of this, the Baja missions thrived. The Spanish had outposts in Loreto and La Paz. The Jesuits even planned to expand their string of missions up to San Diego.

Then, in the 1760s, the situation changed. First, King

Eusebio Francisco Kino was born on August 10, 1645, in Segno, Tirol. (Tirol is now a part of Italy.) He went to school in Germany. He became famous as a mathematician and astronomer.

In 1665, he entered the Society of Jesus. This order of priests is also called the Jesuits. Kino became very ill in 1673 and nearly died. He believed that God had spared him, a belief that inspired him to become a missionary.

In 1681, he got his chance. Kino joined a 100-man expedition to Baja California. Spain had been trying to establish a colony there. At that point, it had only met with failure. The expedition prepared for travel and arrived in Baja in 1683. There, they started a colony at La Paz.

Despite his illness, Kino was ruggedly built. He and his friend, Juan Maria Salvaterria, traveled north of La Paz. Kino marched tirelessly, exploring for days on end.

The colony at La Paz faced starvation for its first two years. Eventually, it was abandoned. Only Kino and Salvaterria stayed behind. Without the presence of the town, Kino moved further north. He founded Nuestra Senora de los Dolores (Our Lady of the Sorrowful), the first mission among Indians in the region. In his travels, he introduced wheat to Pima Indian farmers and opposed the slavery of Indians in silver mines. The trail he walked became known as *El Camino del Diablo* – The Devil's Road.

Moving north, Father Kino discovered the end of the Sea of Cortés. This was important, since it meant that California was not an island. Kino established 29 missions before his death, and in 1705 drew the first map that accurately depicted Baja California as a peninsula connected to Alta California. He died on March 15, 1711, in Magdalena, Mexico.

When King Charles III took the throne in Spain, the course of history for the missions took an interesting twist. He replaced the Jesuit missionaries with Franciscan friars.

Charles III came to power in 1759. He disliked the Jesuits. He took control of the Pious Fund and ejected the Jesuits from Spain. He sent José de Gálvez to clear them from the colonies. This left the Jesuit missions without priests. So, Charles charged the Franciscan order of **friars** to continue the Jesuits' work. Franciscan padre Junipero Serra was appointed father president of the missions in Baja.

Soon afterward, Russian fur trappers were spotted near San Francisco. They were hunting seal and otters on the Farallone Islands. This was much further south than they had ever gone before. To protect the Spanish claim, King Charles ordered the colonization of Alta California. As in Baja, these colonies would begin as missions. The final era of Spanish colonialism was about to begin.

TWO SEEDS OF COLONIZATION

JOSÉ DE GÁLVEZ, THE VISITADOR GENERAL OF NEW SPAIN, ACTED QUICKLY. KING CHARLES HAD ordered him to colonize Alta California. He first contacted Father Serra, who would found the missions to begin the colony. Captain Gaspar de Portola would be the military leader.

Colonists left in four waves. Two ships left, followed by two groups on land. The first group, sailing in the *San Carlos*, left La Paz on January 9, 1769. The second, in the *San Antonio*, left on February 15. Both ships used bad maps. On their charts, the port was 100 miles north of its actual position. The *San Antonio* arrived on April 11, after 55 days at sea. The *San Carlos*, which had left first, showed up two weeks later. Storms had blown it 200 miles off course. When the *San*

Jesuit missionaries preach to the Native Americans, hoping to attract them to mission life. Once the Spanish controlled some of the California coast, they believed it necessary to enrich the Indian ways with their own.

As missionaries came to California, be it by ship or by land, they found the journey difficult. One of their biggest enemies was scurvy, a disease that results from a bad diet and attacks the muscles and joints. Fruits and vegetables will combat the disease, but a lack of good food caused many missionaries to die from scurvy.

Carlos finally dropped anchor, its sailors had not set foot on land for 110 days.

The journey was hard. Of the 90 sailors, only 30 survived the trip. Many soldiers were dead as well. The main killer of these men was **scurvy**. Scurvy is a disease caused by a bad diet. It rots the gums and attacks the muscles and joints. It's curable with fruits and vegetables, but there were none aboard the ship. None were growing in San Diego, either. The colonists remained gravely ill. Many died even after they reached land.

On May 14, the first of two caravans arrived. It was the cattle drive, led by Captain Fernando de Rivera. Many of these settlers were sick and hungry as well. Serra and Portola's journey to San Diego was not much easier. They took 45 days to travel 350 miles. Of the two land expeditions, half of the travelers never reached San Diego. Many died along the way, while others deserted the group.

Serra and Portola arrived in San Diego on July 1. They weren't greeted by a bustling colony in progress. Instead, San Diego seemed more like a hospital in a war zone.

 José de Gálvez was born in 1720, in Velez-Malaga, Spain. His family was poor. Still, he attended the University of Salamanca. He graduated with a doctorate in law.

Gálvez was a talented lawyer. He attracted the attention of Spain's King, Charles III. Charles put Gálvez on the Council of the Indies. The council directed Spain's colonies, including those in the New World.

In 1765, King Charles sent Gálvez to New Spain. His title was "visitador general." He would supervise the colony's government. His first job was to evict the Jesuits from the colonies. Gálvez quieted any protestors with force. Gálvez also reorganized the colonial tax system and gave the government a monopoly on tobacco.

In 1769, Gálvez contacted Captain Gaspar de Portola and Father Junipero Serra. He had picked them to lead a colony into Alta California. There, Father Serra would start two missions. Gálvez stayed behind to govern Mexico. It was probably for the best. Gálvez was a master at cutting through Spanish red tape. In order to get anything done, the missions needed him to communicate with Spain.

Eventually, Gálvez returned to Spain. He was promoted to minister of the Indies, and remained in charge of the missions from Spain. He was granted the title of marquis of Sonora in 1785. He died two years later.

Nonetheless, Father Serra noted the beauty of the region. He wrote, "Thanks be to God. I arrived here at the Port of San Diego. It is beautiful to behold, and does not belie its reputation."

👆 This shrine can be found along a road near La Paz, in Baja California. The elaborate ornamentation of the cactus "cross" is typical of the style of the Southwest.

The journey was over, and the hard work of survival had begun. After more scurvy deaths, there were eight remaining sailors. Captain Portola ordered them to sail for San Blas in the *San Antonio*. They could pick up supplies and bring them to the mission. Until they returned, the colonists would have to make do with what they had.

The colonists expected another supply ship. It was to bring dried meat, dried figs, wine, brandy, raisins, dried fish, church bells, **vestments**, and trading materials. It never came. The ship, called the *San Jose*, was sent out twice. The first time, it returned to La Paz after three months at sea. It left again the next spring, and was never seen again.

Within two weeks of his arrival, Father Serra had erected a cross. He put it on a hill overlooking the bay. Serra said his first **Mass** there on July 16. Later that day, Captain Portola and his 40 healthiest men set out for Monterey. Father Serra's childhood friend, Father Juan Crespi, left with him.

In truth, Monterey was Spain's true goal. It was close enough to San Francisco to keep the Russians away. San Diego was the crucial halfway point between Monterey and Baja. Without San Diego, a colony as far away as Monterey would never have a chance.

Soon after Portola left, Father Serra made contact with the Ipai and Tipai Indians. They were the natives of San Diego. At this time, the native population of California was more than 300,000 people. It was the most densely populated area of what became the United States. Most Indians in the area lived in small villages. Each "tribelet" had about 100 to 500 people. Sometimes a village would honor the leader of a central village as its chief. In these cases, the chief had mostly ceremonial power. Other leaders were the shaman, and the heads of the village's families.

Father Serra tried to befriend the Indians. He offered them gifts, and food. The Indians gladly accepted beads and other trinkets. However, they would not touch Serra's food. They believed the Spaniards' food to be spoiled and the reason why so many of them were sick.

Captain Portola's trek to Monterey was faring no better than his march to San Diego. He and his men were starving. Eventually, the soldiers had to eat a pack mule each day. The meat smelled bad when it was cooking, and it tasted no better. To make matters worse, earthquakes would sometimes spook the livestock they were herding. Each time, Portola and his men rounded up the horses, mules, and other animals. This cost them precious time.

When Portola and his men reached a large, sheltered bay, they knew it was too far north to be Monterey. Portola thought the bay was one that had been discovered nearly 200 years earlier and named for St. Francis by a Spanish priest aboard a galleon. Even when the Spaniards realized that this was an error, the name—San Francisco—stuck.

The trail seemed to go on forever. Portola searched for the beautiful, sheltered port of Monterey that Captain Vizcaino had described. It was nowhere to be found. Finally, Father Crespi erected a cross. The group prayed for guidance, and moved on. On November 7, they recognized San Francisco Bay. They had traveled too far. Tired and hungry, they began walking back to San Diego. Near San Luis Obispo, Portola organized a hunt. The group shot and ate several grizzly bears.

Gaspar de Portola was born in 1723, the son of a noble family in Balaguer, Spain. Portola joined the Spanish army at age 11. He rose in rank to lieutenant, and then to captain. He fought in battles against Portugal and Italy.

In 1767, Portola was appointed Governor of the Californias. Since there were no Spanish settlements in Alta California, his initial charge was governing Baja California. One of his first acts was to expel the Society of Jesus from Baja California. His orders came from King Charles III and José de Gálvez.

Two years later, Gálvez named Portola for an important job. Captain Portola was ordered to lead an expedition to Alta California. There, he would begin missions and colonies with Father Junipero Serra. Portola helped found a colony at San Diego. Two weeks later, he left with 40 men in search of Monterey. On his first journey, he marched as far north as San Francisco. He thought he missed Monterey. After six months, he returned to San Diego in defeat. He later returned to Monterey, and founded a colony there.

In 1770, Portola stepped down as governor of California. In 1776, he became mayor of Puebla, Mexico. He retired in 1784, and returned to Spain. Portola died within the year.

Portola's crew returned to San Diego on January 24 and discussed their six-month trek with Father Serra. Serra realized that the harbor where they put their cross was, in truth, Monterey. "You come from Rome," exclaimed Father Serra, "and you did not see the Pope!"

Even knowing this, nothing could be done. The mission was running out of food quickly. The priests and soldiers were

The work of the missionaries was far from humble, and they constructed buildings to match. This illustration shows how a California mission could dominate the surrounding landscape.

not adequate farmers. While some tried planting seeds, the results were meager. Also, none of the Spaniards had the Tipai's talent of foraging for food.

After seven months of starvation and disease, Captain Portola faced a hard truth. They would have to abandon the mission. It was the only way to save the colonists' lives. The **padres** protested, but Portola set a date to leave.

On March 19, people were already packing up to go when a sharp-eyed colonist spotted a ship in the distance. They waited, and on March 23, it arrived. It was the *San Antonio*, loaded with rice, beans, and flour. When the ship had reached San Blas, only two sailors were still alive. Sailing as soon as possible for San Diego, they arrived just in time. The colony was saved.

After regaining some strength, Portola made his way back to Monterey. Father Serra sailed to the port in the *San Antonio*. When they arrived, they saw Father Crespi's cross. It was covered by shells and feathers, and surrounded by arrows in the ground. These were offerings left by the local people who had seen the reverence with which the Spaniards held the cross.

On June 3, 1770, bells were hung in the trees. Father Serra blessed the area. Muskets and cannons were fired from the *San Antonio* during his Mass. The second mission had been founded. The partnership of Christian faith and military force had a foothold in California.

MISSION LIFE

WITH THE FIRST TWO MISSIONS BUILT, SPANISH
COLONIZATION COULD BEGIN, BUT THE PADRES
and soldiers could not colonize Alta California by
themselves. They lacked many useful survival skills, including
farming. They needed others to join them in Alta California
to help the settlement succeed.

The Spanish government tried to encourage settlers. They
gave every colonist a lot for a house and land for farming.
Everyone could use the shared grazing fields. The government
loaned colonists livestock and farm tools. Colonists were paid
$10 a month for the first two years. For the next three, they
would get $5 a month. To top it all off, colonists would pay no
taxes for five years. After that, they would be given the
permanent title to the land they used.

In return, colonists promised to sell their extra food to the

The tiled roofs in the courtyard and tower of a
presidio glisten in the sunlight. Soldiers from the Spanish
government lived in presidios to protect the missions.

Captain Sebastian Vizcaino is responsible for the names of many of the cities in California today. Cities like San Diego, San Francisco, and San Luis Obispo are all named after saints; "san" is the Spanish word for "saint."

presidios. Presidios were forts built to protect the missions. They were in San Diego, San Francisco, Monterey, and Santa Barbara. Colonists had to serve in the town militia and help with community projects. These included digging irrigation ditches and putting up new buildings.

Despite these offers, turnout was low. Alta California was a very dangerous place to live. One group that came was prisoners—many convicts were freed from jail to go to Alta. The tough laws of Spain jailed many harmless people. Not everyone in the jails would be considered a criminal today. Nonetheless, many dangerous men went to Alta. Long-time colonists were usually suspicious of newcomers.

Still, the colonists needed all the help they could get. For years, settlers depended on small supply shipments. Cargo ships could only carry a few months' supplies. Many ships were blown off course. Also, supplies couldn't travel on land. The Spanish feared that the Indians would attack them and steal the shipment.

Father Serra was named father president of the Alta California missions. Captain Portola served as governor briefly but was soon replaced by Don Pedro Fages. Portola then sailed

This portrait of a Native Californian suggests that their appearance was not tremendously exotic. However, their physical appearance and cultural values set them apart from the Spanish settlers.

for Mexico, where his report on the California colony was not optimistic. "The mines of gold and silver and other rich products … we never saw or found, as our first care was to hunt for meat to keep from starving," he wrote. "It [is] impossible to send aid to Monterey by sea, and still more so

The bell tower, or *companario*, of the mission at San Miguel reaches toward the clouds. This structure was one of the most delicately designed portions of a California mission.

by land, unless it was proposed to sacrifice thousands of men and huge sums of money." The good news, however, was that "the natives of California are so gentle that we never had to defend ourselves," Portola wrote.

Serra and Fages started working to settle the 650 miles between San Diego and Monterey. In 1771, they founded the first new mission, San Antonio de Padua.

In 1772, a second **famine** struck. Only another large-scale bear hunt kept the colonies at Monterey and San Antonio de Padua alive. By 1773, there were several other missions in California, including San Diego, San Gabriel, and San Luís Obispo. However, there were only 61 Spanish soldiers and 11 priests living in Alta California. There were no doctors, no farmers, no craftsmen, and no white women. With no easy way to supply the settlements, they were colonies in name only.

The supply problems were solved in 1774. An intelligent soldier named Juan Bautista de Anza, who was in charge of the presidio at Tubac in present-day Arizona, asked the king for permission to establish a trade route between his outpost and the Spanish mission at Monterey. Anza and a priest named Francisco Garcés explored the great western desert with a group of 20 men. After three months, they arrived at the San Gabriel mission. From there he traveled to Monterey.

Anza soon returned to his own fort, accompanied by a number of Pedro Fages's soldiers from Monterey, who marked the trail. The next year, Anza assembled a larger expedition,

Father Junipero Serra was born in Majorca, Spain, on November 24, 1713. When he was 17, he entered the Franciscan order. Eight years later, he was ordained as a priest. Father Serra earned a doctorate at Lullian University in Palma. He taught philosophy there for 15 years.

In 1749, Father Serra became a missionary. He sailed to Mexico, landing in Vera Cruz. Upon landing, he felt he had to do penance, so he walked 550 miles, from Vera Cruz to Mexico City. During the walk, a spider bit him. Its venom crippled his leg. Walking was difficult for the rest of his life.

Father Serra finally arrived in Mexico City on New Year's Day, 1750. His first missionary work was at a mission called Sierra Gorda.

made up of Spanish families from Mexico who wished to settle in California. He set out with 240 people, many of them women and children, along with nearly 700 horses and 355 head of cattle. In March 1776, he arrived at Monterey, where the settlers ended their journey. Anza continued north to San Francisco Bay, and in September 1776 he selected the site for a Spanish fort and mission on the bay.

In Monterey, Governor Fages and Father Serra clashed on many issues. Technically, the governor was in charge in all

It was a very tough outpost. Serra served there for eight years and spent the next nine in southern Mexico.

In 1767, the Society of Jesus, another order of priests, was expelled from Baja California. The Franciscans took over their missions, and Father Serra was put in charge of the missions at Baja. Soon, however, he got orders that would change his life. He was to found missions in Alta California.

Serra founded nine missions in all. His first two were at San Diego and Monterey in 1769 and 1770. San Antonio (1771), San Gabriel (1771), San Luis Obispo (1772), San Juan Capistrano (1775), San Francisco (1776), Santa Clara (1777), and San Buenaventura (1782) followed. For his service, Father Serra was named the apostle of California.

People are divided on Serra's reputation. His biographer, Francisco Palou, wrote about Serra so glowingly that it is difficult to get a clear picture of him. Some consider Serra a firm defender of Indians' rights on the missions. However, others say the native mission workers were treated like slaves under his watch.

Father Serra died in 1784. He was beatified on September 28, 1988.

matters except spiritual. But the religious nature of the missions blurred these distinctions. Both Fages and Serra tried to take charge.

For instance, Serra wanted a mission at Ventura, but Fages vetoed the idea. He thought the mission would be too hard to defend. The mission was delayed for 10 years. In the meantime, other missions were built. Between 1772 and 1776, Serra founded three more missions between Monterey and San Diego. At one point, Fages wrote that Serra's urge to start new missions was "nothing less than the temptation of the evil one."

Eventually, Father Serra traveled to Mexico City to present his case for the Ventura mission. He was convincing. Governor Fages was swiftly replaced, and San Buenaventura was founded in 1782. Still, the tension between priest and presidio remained.

Padres saw the missions' purpose as spreading Christianity. The government saw them as a cheap way to colonize. The Spanish government was poor. It used the Jesuits' Pious Fund to found the missions. The fund paid each padre about $300 in goods. Also, each mission received $1,000 to start. This paid for bells, vestments, tools, seeds, and other needs.

Spain had trouble keeping the colonies supplied, so the missions began trading with ships from New England. This was against the law, but the missionaries didn't have much choice. American ships brought tools, furniture, glass, cookware, and musical instruments. Soon, more traders started making the trip to California. Business at the missions boomed.

At the missions, Indians worked with no pay. Instead, the mission land was held "in trust" to the native people. With converted Indians as free labor, the missions soon were self-supporting. The missionaries promised the Indians Spanish citizenship. They tried to mold the Indians into Spaniards. This process is called **acculturation**. (The Spaniards would call it "civilizing" the Indians.) It was supposed to take 10 years. After that, the missionaries would move on. The natives would run their own town, and pay taxes to Spain. This was the

Spanish plan. The reality of the missions was different.

To start a new mission, two padres would be assigned. One would be in charge of spiritual matters, and the other would take care of the mission business. The duties often overlapped.

First, the padres would choose a site. Mission buildings looked very similar. Missions usually had a rectangular courtyard called a quadrangle. An outdoor hallway, called a *corredor*, bordered the quadrangle. Surrounding it were several rooms. These included the workshop, the priests' living quarters, the cooking area, a dormitory, and the chapel. The chapel would be in the northeast corner. The front wall of the chapel would often stand higher than the rest of the building. There would be gaps in the wall to hang the church bells. This wall of bells was called the *campanario*.

New missions needed to attract Indians' attention, so priests would hang bells in the trees. Curious Indians would investigate the strange music. From there, the padres tried to earn their trust. They gave the Indians gifts, such as glass beads, clothing, blankets, or food.

Once the padres were trusted, they tried to convert the natives to Christianity. It was a slow process, but the padres were convincing. Converted Indians were called **neophytes**. Neophyte is a Latin word that means, "newly planted." In the first 5 years of the missions, there were 462 conversions. A total of 491 babies were baptized, and 62 couples were married. Neophytes attended church services several times a day. Once an Indian was converted, he couldn't leave the mission without permission.

The missionaries expected the neophytes to have children. The children would be the beginning of a new, Christian population. However, the Indian population didn't grow inside the missions—it declined. From 1779 to 1833, there were 29,000 Indian births, but 62,000 Indians died during the same time period.

This was strange. As a whole, the Indians were a very healthy group. In Santa Barbara, nearly 5,000 adults were baptized. Only 30 were ill in any serious way. However, the native Californians had no immunity to the European diseases. They caught smallpox and measles from the Spanish. A measles epidemic killed a third of all Indian children in 1806. In San Francisco, the disease killed 880 children. This nearly wiped out an entire generation.

As the missions continued, padres were under pressure to keep their population up. Since few babies were born, they needed converts. In some cases, the conversions were not voluntary. One ex-neophyte, a Kamia Indian named Janitin, remembered his "conversion." He and his relatives were catching clams along the beach. Two men on horseback rode near. Janitin and his family ran. "It was too late," remembers Janitin. "They overtook me and lassoed and dragged me for a long distance."

At the mission, Janitin was locked up for a week. He was told he would be converted. "One day they threw water on my head and gave me salt to eat, and with this the interpreter told me that now I was a Christian and that I was called Jesus."

The missions set up schools, to teach neophytes to read and write Spanish. At first, the padres tried to teach them to read and write in their own languages. They didn't realize the native Californians spoke 80 different languages, which was was too many for the padres to handle.

Most Indians were taught how to farm. Missions grew fruits and vegetables, as well as corn, barley, wheat, and pinto beans.

Some Indians were also trained in a craft. Men learned blacksmithing, tanning, and winemaking. Women learned cooking, sewing, spinning, and weaving. Many Indians were talented craftsmen before the Spaniards came. For example, the Chumash Indians near Santa Barbara built excellent plank boats. They were quick and very well made, and would hold 10 to 12 people. These crafts were ignored in favor of Spanish tasks, and mission workers struggled to meet high daily quotas.

To keep control, the missionaries set up many rules. Neophytes would be whipped or jailed if they disobeyed. Women and children would be beaten on occasion. A neophyte named Lorenzo Asisana remembered, "We were always trembling with fear of the lash."

One friar, visiting Mission San Miguel, wrote, "The treatment shown to the Indians is the most cruel I have ever read in history. For the slightest things they receive heavy floggings, are shackled, and put in the stocks, and treated with so much cruelty that they are kept whole days without a drink of water." After making this complaint, the friar was declared insane. He was taken out of Alta California by armed guards.

Children in the mission also led changed lives. At just five or six years old, most children were taken from their families. They lived in a dorm-like barracks that was also their school. This accomplished two things. First, it helped acculturate the children. Without their parents near, they would not learn the old tribal ways. Second, it meant that the parents could not turn against the mission. Although it probably remained unspoken, the children were always potential hostages.

Girls and young women were also kept apart. When they got married, they joined their husbands. If he died, they would be locked up again. Single women were a source of conflict and therefore a danger.

Five or six soldiers guarded each mission. They were often used as bosses to supervise Indian work crews. To help the guards keep order, padres appointed neophyte police. More troops could be brought in from nearby presidios if they were needed.

Neophytes and missionaries ate three meals a day when there was food. A 1773 agreement made the missions responsible for feeding the presidio. Soldiers were fed mostly wheat, while the Indians ate mostly corn. The soldiers received their food first, so the Indians were hurt by a lean harvest more than the presidio. This unequal treatment strained their relationship, but it wouldn't be the only thing to do so.

👆 A bell hangs outside Mission San Francisco Solano, ready to call neophytes to worship. Most of the Spanish missions still stand today and remind us of their unique histories.

RESISTANCE

AS THE MISSIONS PROGRESSED, THE FRAGILE CHURCH AND GOVERNMENT PARTNERSHIP WAS uneasy. One cause of this was the presidio soldiers. Soldiers were often drunk or rowdy, and many assaulted native women. This caused the Indians to strike back. These conflicts made the priest's jobs harder.

Still, the governor wouldn't punish the soldiers, because he couldn't risk them deserting the mission. The colony couldn't survive without them. To ease tensions, the padres moved the missions away from the soldiers' barracks. They hoped the Indians would see a difference between them and the soldiers.

The missions continued to grow and change. In 1784, Father Serra died. He was briefly replaced by his biographer, Father Francisco Palou. Much of what we know of the early mission era comes from Palou's writing. After a year, a permanent replacement was found. Father Fermin de Lasuen was a troubleshooter at several missions. His work helped keep the peace with Indians at San Gabriel, San Diego, and San Carlos. He would lead the missions for 19 years. Under Lasuen, the number of missions in Alta California grew to 18. Lasuen also changed what the mission buildings looked

The mission style of building, which features curved roof tiles and wide arches, became popular in California in the late 1800s for a variety of buildings, especially homes. It was patterned after a style used to build Spanish missions, which is where it got its name.

like. He introduced rounded roof tiles and wide arches to missions he founded. He also replaced the thatched roofs of early missions with tiles. This building style was so distinct it is now known as the **"mission style."**

Father Lasuen died in 1804. In the last 31 years of the missions, only three more missions were added. The last was San Francisco Solano, founded in 1823. This brought the chain of missions to 21.

Throughout the mission era, many Indians resisted the missionaries. Their resistance took on many forms. Many Indians were outwardly helpful. They let their dislike of the church come through in quiet way: some simply did slow or sloppy work; many refused to learn Spanish; others learned, but pretended not to understand it; some sneaked Indian religious symbols into their work; and secret rituals were held to reverse baptisms.

Other Indians ran away from the missions. Some left on foot, while others stole horses. Once beyond the mission, they encountered problems. The padres knew their home villages. They would know to look for them there. Most other villages

👆 The padres who came to the California coast for mission life had few luxuries. This priest's room at San Juan Capistrano mission reveals the bare, unadorned existence they led in the New World.

would not take a stranger in because many neophytes carried deadly European diseases, and soldiers dealt harshly with towns that hid fugitives. Recaptured Indians were flogged and put in the stocks for days.

Some Indians would be even bolder in their resistance. Pomponio, a Coastal Miwok Indian, and Estanislao, a Northern Valley Yokut, led horse-stealing rings. This was unusual, since horses were new to the Indians. Horses were valued in part because of the missions' overall goal.

The missions were supposed to make Indians into Spanish citizens. In order to do this, the Native Americans had to know horsemanship. Spain had a law against Indians riding horses, and the penalty was death. In spite of this, neophytes were taught horse-breeding, branding, and riding. Some of these Indians ran away, and taught horsemanship to their free tribesmen. Soon, California Indians were among the best riders in the West. At their peak, Indian horse thieves stole thousands of horses a month.

Other neophytes used poison. In 1801, four padres were poisoned in Mission San Miguel. One died. Another padre died of poison at San Diego in 1811. The next year, in Mission Santa Cruz, some neophytes smothered and mutilated a padre. He had unveiled a new device to use for discipline, and the Indians saw it as torture.

Even after the missions had closed, former neophytes took revenge. In 1836, Cahuilla Indians kidnapped some padres. They horsewhipped them in return for years at the padres' lash.

The tensions between the Indians and the Spanish made for a dangerous climate. Padres could not leave the missions without armed guards. Soldiers regularly fought Indians near the San Joaquin River. These Indians attacked neophytes and encouraged runaways and revolts.

Not all resistance to the missions was on a small scale. The history of the missions is riddled with organized native uprisings. The first happened in November 1775. One thousand Kumeyaay warriors attacked the San Diego mission. They set the mission itself on fire. In the battle, they killed a priest, a blacksmith, and a carpenter. One of the Kumeyaay also died in the attack. Eventually, the Spanish drove them back, and the priests moved to the presidio for six months.

In 1781, Quechan Indians destroyed two new missions along the Colorado River in Baja California. They killed 55 colonists—four padres, 31 soldiers, and 20 civilians. Plus, they cut off a land route between Alta California and Mexico.

The Mission at San Gabriel also had a large revolt. San Gabriel was located at a mission crossroads. Soldiers were always passing through, and they often caused trouble. One soldier assaulted the local chief's wife. The chief attacked the soldiers and was killed. His head was put on a stake at the presidio. This stirred bad blood between the Indians and the colonists. Fathers Paterna and Crusado's careful treatment of the

Fermin Francisco de Lasuen was born in Victoria, Spain, on June 7, 1736. When he was still very young, he joined the Franciscan order of priests. In 1759, he sailed to Mexico to be a missionary. His first station was the Sierra Gorda mission, where Father Junipero Serra began his missionary career. After eight years, Lasuen moved on to the Baja missions.

In 1773, Father Lasuen traveled north to Alta California. Lasuen would solve problems at troubled missions. He eased conflicts with the tribes in San Diego and San Gabriel. He was a well-liked and capable missionary.

1n 1785, Father Lasuen followed in Father Serra's footsteps once again. He was named father president of the California missions. There were nine active missions when Lasuen took over. He added nine more before his death. His first new missions were Santa Barbara (1786), La Purisima (1787), Santa Cruz (1791), and Soledad (1791). In 1797, he founded five at once. They were rest stops for traveling between the major missions. These were San Jose, San Juan Bautista, San Miguel, San Fernando, and San Luis Rey.

In his 18 years heading the missions, Lasuen increased the importance of livestock. Also, he changed the style of mission architecture into what we know today. He added wide arches and rounded tiles to the roofs.

Father Lasuen was a talented man who brought much to the missions. He died in 1804. He is buried at San Carlos de Borromeo in Carmel, his home base as president.

Indians brought back some trust. Eventually, the slaughtered chief's son was even baptized. Still, tensions remained high.

In 1785, a medicine woman named Toypurina led a revolt against the mission. Eventually, it was put down, and Toypurina was arrested. At her trial, she said, "I hate the padres and all of you for living here on my native soil...for trespassing on the lands of my forefathers and despoiling our tribal domains."

The Indians weren't the only ones fighting Spanish rule. From 1810 to 1821, Mexicans fought for their independence. In 1821, they finally got it. Alta California was now ruled by Mexico. The revolution confused the chain of command. The missions faced several small revolutions and Indian uprisings.

The biggest of these happened in 1824. The Chumash people at Santa Barbara, San Ines, and La Purisma all rose up against the missionaries. After the battles, Indians from Santa Barbara and San Ines fled to La Purisma. Once there, they grabbed whatever guns and cannons they could find. Mexican soldiers surrounded La Purisma. The Indians held them off for a month. Even after a long siege, some Indians refused to surrender. About half of the Indians from these missions fled east, to the interior of California.

Under Mexican rule, supplies and funds could not be counted on. The missions had to work harder to support themselves and the military. The end of the mission era was near. In 15 years, it would all be over.

🔥 American Navy planes form a cross as they fly over the Santa Barbara mission in California. As the importance of the missions declined early in the 19th century, the Franciscans abandoned the missions.

THE MISSION ERA ENDS

IN 1833, THE MEXICAN GOVERNMENT BEGAN TO TAKE CONTROL OF THE MISSIONS. THE MISSIONS had grown as businesses. They owned thousands of cattle, horses, and other livestock. Their farms harvested tons of grain. This was worth a lot of money to Mexico.

The Mexican government claimed half of the missions' property. It set the other half aside for the Indians. This process was called **secularization**. The mission lands were divided in various ways. The Catholic Church kept the chapel, the padres' apartments, and their gardens. The rest of the mission building housed public services for the town. A large area was set aside for public farming. Each Indian family was granted a plot of the remaining land. There were 30,000 Indians associated with the missions. Each grant was enough for a small house and some light farming. This was a big change. Before secularization, there were only 21 privately owned plots of land in California. Now, there were thousands.

The Franciscans tried to make as much money as possible before the government came. They planned to split it with the

As part of the acculturation process, Indian children in missions were often separated from their parents at a young age, so they wouldn't be influenced by the family's traditions and culture.

Indians. Missionaries at Santa Barbara killed thousands of cattle to sell the hides. The Mexican governor had to work quickly to seize the mission land. He claimed more than 600,000 cows, burning them with Mexico's brand.

Mission San Gabriel was devastated by secularization. It had been one of the richest missions. The padre in charge turned over all of the mission's wealth to the government for distribution. A corrupt official left nothing for the friars and Indians.

Priests reacted to the change differently. Many padres broke their vows and misused their power. Others remained committed to the Indians. Father Vicente Sarria begged in the streets for Indian children. He kept nothing for himself. He eventually starved to death.

The Indians fared no better. Most never placed much importance on personal property. Many did not realize what their land grants meant. Developers swindled them out of their land. Some Indians gambled their deeds away.

Soon, the developers had plenty of land. They built large work farms called ranchos. They took up the mission's businesses. Many Indians, seeing no other option, went to work for the ranchos. Unlike the priests, the ranchers had no

No Christian mission was complete without a cross. Another common ornamentation was a votive picture of the Virgin Mary, which was usually placed near the altar inside a mission church.

sense of Christian charity and duty. Native Americans at ranchos lived in even worse conditions than at the missions.

Not all the ex-neophytes worked on the ranchos. Some became guides for travelers. Many others headed east, to the interior of California. There they hoped to resume their traditional way of life. Converted Indians were welcomed back to the tribes. The natives now knew the threat that Europeans posed because the neophytes had valuable information on the enemy.

Unfortunately, the California ecosystem had changed drastically in 70 years. Indians had stolen Spanish animals like the horse, and many ran free. Their grazing destroyed fragile California plant life. This hurt the environment badly. Most Indians could no longer live off the land. There were exceptions, however—at San Luis Rey, 200 former neophytes flourished in Temecula Valley. Nonetheless, nine out of 10 neophytes died within 15 years.

In the 1850s and 1860s, the U.S. Federal Land commission returned some mission land to the Catholic Church. By then, the chapels and quadrangles were too large for religious services, so the church leased the buildings out. The San Fernando mission spent some time as a pig farm. The mission at San Juan Capistrano stored hay.

During the 1860s, newcomers to California began building in the mission style. This style lasted through the 1900s. The interest also sparked the restoration of the original missions. Unfortunately, many missions were rebuilt without attention to their former design. Elements of New England churches mixed with the arches and tiled roofs. The results were unsatisfying. Thankfully, later restorations have been more faithful. Many have even undone the "improvements" of earlier years.

To look back on the mission system is to understand how good intentions can go wrong. Many padres were devoted to the neophytes of their mission. They thought they were saving the Indians' souls. They believed their work was meaningful and important.

Also, the Spanish wanted to train the Californians for a "better" way of life. The missionaries planned to return the land to the Indians. They had done this in Baja California, and expected to in Alta as well. They wanted the Indians to eventually govern their own villages, under Spanish rule.

Yet, despite their intentions, the plan failed. In the 65 years of the California mission system, no group of neophytes was left to govern itself. Instead, Indians

While they may have been working together to establish missions in California, the government and religious interests were doing it for different reasons. The Catholic Church saw is as a opportunity to spread Christianity in the New World, while the government saw it as a cheap way to colonize.

continued to work for no pay. They could not come and go as they pleased. They were punished harshly, to the point of torture. To an Indian, the missions were run like slave camps.

To make matters worse, Spanish culture was forced on the Indians. Their own traditions were wiped out, and much of their population was also destroyed by disease and exhaustion. In very real ways, the Spanish brought death.

By modern standards, the missions seem cruel, even evil. It's important to remember that these deeds were performed with good, if misguided, intentions. Only then can forgiveness occur and centuries-old wounds begin to heal.

GLOSSARY

Acculturation

The process of acclimating a person of one culture into another culture, as the Spaniards tried to do to the Indians.

Alta California

During the mission era, upper California was called Alta California.

Baja California

During the mission era, lower California was called Baja California.

Colony

A land that is claimed for and under the reign of a faraway government.

Famine

A period in which food is scarce, causing many people to starve.

Friar

A member of a religious order, such as those that operated Spanish missions.

Jesuits

An order of priests also known as the Order of Jesus.

Mass

A celebration that constitutes the service of the Catholic Church.

Missionary

A person sent by a religious group to spread its faith or carry on its work.

Mission style

A style of building that features rounded roof tiles and wide arches, as were used in Spanish missions.

Neophyte

Indians who were converted to Christianity were called neophytes.

Padre

A priest.

Presidio

Forts that were built to protect the Spanish missions.

Scurvy

A disease caused by a bad diet that attacks the muscles and joints, sometimes leading to death.

Secularization

The process of splitting the mission property between the government and the Indians at the end of the mission era.

Vestments

Ceremonial robes or garments, often worn by religious leaders.

Viceroy

Officials who governed the Spanish colonies in California.

TIMELINE

1542
Juan Rodriguez Cabrillo maps the California coast.

1579
Francis Drake encounters some Miwok Indians at San Francisco.

1602
Sebastian Vizcaino names California ports and bays. He flatters the Count of Monte Rey with an inaccurate description of Monterey.

1690s
Father Eusebio Francisco Kino discovers California is not an island.

1749
Father Junipero Serra sails to New Spain and walks from Vera Cruz to Mexico City. A spider bites his leg, crippling him.

1759
Charles III becomes king of Spain

1767
Charles III evicts Jesuits from Spanish colonies. He sends José de Gálvez to the colonies as Visitador General.

1769
Father Serra and Captain Gaspar de Portola found the Californias' first mission in San Diego. Portola searches for Monterey.

1770
Serra and Portola found a mission in Monterey. Portola steps down as governor. He is replaced by Don Pedro Fages.

1771
Missions San Antonio and San Miguel are founded.

1772
Mission San Luis Obispo is founded. Famine ends with a bear hunt.

1773
Father Fermin Lasuen joins Alta California missions.

1774
Juan Bautista de Anza finds new land route for supplies.

1775
Mission San Diego is attacked by 1,000 Kumeyaay warriors. San Juan Capistrano is founded.

1776
Mission San Francisco is founded. The American Revolution begins.

1777
Mission Santa Clara is founded.

1781
Quechan Indians destroy two missions in Baja California, killing 55 colonists.

1782
Father Serra convinces the government to support San Buenaventura. Governor Fages is replaced.

1784
Father Serra dies. Father Francisco Palou becomes father president until a replacement is found.

1785
Father Fermin Lasuen becomes father president of the missions. He changes the design of new missions, and increases the importance of livestock. Toypurina leads a revolt against Mission San Gabriel.

1786
Father Lasuen founds Mission Santa Barbara.

1787
Mission La Purisima is founded.

1791
Mission Santa Cruz and Mission Soledad are founded.

1797
Missions founded at San Jose, San Juan Batista, San Miguel, San Fernando, and San Luis Rey.

1804
Father Fermin dies. Mission Santa Ines is founded.

1810
War for Mexican Independence begins.

1817
Mission San Rafael is founded.

1821
Mexico wins its independence from Spain. Alta California changes hands.

1823
The last of the missions, Mission San Francisco Solano, is founded.

1824
Revolts occur at Santa Barbera, San Ines, and La Purisma. Indians take over La Purisma, and hold the army off for a month.

1833–1834
Mexican government secularizes missions of California. Mission era ends.

FURTHER READING

Bec, Warren A., and Williams, David A. *California: A History of the Golden State*. Garden City, N.Y.: Doubleday and Company, 1972.

Cary, Diana Serra. "California Indians on the White man's Frontier," *Wild West* 12, no. 2. (August 1999).

Champagne, Duane. *Native America: Portrait of the Peoples*. Detroit, Mich.: Visible Ink Press, 1994.

Isaacs, Sally Senzell. *Daily Life in a California Mission*. Crystal Lake, Ill.: Heinemann Library, 2001.

Josephy, Alvin M. Jr. *500 Nations*. New York: Alfred A. Knopf, 1994.

Milanich, Jerald T. *Laboring in the Fields of the Lord: Spanish Missions and Southeastern Indians*. Washington, D.C.: Smithsonian Institution Press, 1999.

Nelson, Libby, and Cornell, Kari. *Projects and Layouts for California Missions*. Minneapolis, Minn.: Lerner Publications, 1998.

Riesenberg, Felix Jr. *The Golden Road*. New York: McGraw-Hill Book Company, 1962.

Shangle, Barbara. *Spanish Missions*. New York: Amer Products, 1997.

Sunset Books. *The California Missions: A Pictorial History*. Menlo Park, Calif.: Lane Book Company, 1964.

Young, Stanley, and Levick, Melba. *The Missions of California*. San Francisco, Calif.: Chronicle Books, 1988.

INTERNET RESOURCES

Spanish Missions outside of California

http://www.lsjunction.com/facts/missions.htm

http://www.cviog.uga.edu/Projects/gainfo/missions.htm

http://www.nps.gov/saan/

http://members.aol.com/jeworth/gbomiss.htm

Spanish Missions of California

http://library.thinkquest.org/3615/

http://www.oneonta.edu/jacksorh/paper2.html

http://www.caohwy.com/m/missions.htm

http://www.bgmm.com/missions/

http://www.geocities.com/TheTropics/6788/missions.html

http://www.ca-missions.org/links.html

The Natives of California

http://www.thehistorynet.com/WildWest/articles/1999/0899_text.html

INDEX

PHOTO CREDITS

ABOUT THE AUTHOR

Rob Staeger lives and writes near Philadelphia. A former newspaper editor, he has written many short stories for young people and several plays for older ones. He has also written a juvenile biography of Wyatt Earp.